HISTORY'S MOST INFLUENTIAL WRITERS

FROM THE Mid-1800s TO THE Late 1800s

Walt Whitman to Anton Chekhov

EDITED BY J.E. LUEBERING

Britannica® Educational Publishing

IN ASSOCIATION WITH

ROSEN EDUCATIONAL SERVICES

Published in 2025 by Britannica Educational Publishing
(a trademark of Encyclopædia Britannica, Inc.)
in association with Rosen Educational Services, LLC
2544 Clinton Street, Buffalo, NY 14224.

Distributed exclusively by Rosen Educational Services.
For a listing of additional Britannica Educational Publishing titles, call toll free (800) 237-9932.

First Edition

Britannica Educational Publishing
Michael I. Levy: Executive Editor
Marilyn L. Barton: Senior Coordinator, Production Control
Steven Bosco: Director, Editorial Technologies
Lisa S. Braucher: Senior Producer and Data Editor
Yvette Charboneau: Senior Copy Editor
Kathy Nakamura: Manager, Media Acquisition
J. E. Luebering: Manager and Senior Editor, Literature

Editor: Greg Roza
Book design: Michael Flynn

Photo credits: Cover https://commons.wikimedia.org/wiki/File:Mark_Twain,_1909.jpg; p. 11 Everett Collection/Shutterstock.com; p. 19 https://commons.wikimedia.org/wiki/File:%C3%89tienne_Carjat,_Portrait_of_Charles_Baudelaire,_circa_1862.jpg.

Cataloging-in-Publication Data

Names: Luebering, J.E.
Title: From the mid-1800s to the late 1800s: Walt Whitman to Anton Chekhov / edited by J.E. Luebering.
Description: New York : Britannica Educational Publishing, in Association with Rosen Educational Services, 2025. | Series: History's most influential writers | Includes glossary and index.
Identifiers: ISBN 9781641901116 (library bound) | ISBN 9781641901109 (pbk) | ISBN 9781641901123 (ebook)
Subjects: LCSH: Authors--19th century--Biography. | Authorship--History--19th century.
Classification: LCC PN451.F766 2025 | DDC 809'.03 B --dc23

Manufactured in the United States of America

CPSIA Compliance Information: Batch #CSBRIT25. For further information contact Rosen Publishing at 1-800-237-9932.

CONTENTS

INTRODUCTION

"Writing is easy. All you have to do is cross out the wrong words."
—Mark Twain (1835–1910)

Open a book—any book. In it you'll find words, of course, but look closely and you'll also find art, crafted, in detail, by a writer proud enough to sign his or her name to the work. In a book, or in any piece of writing, words are joined together at the whim of the author. Sentences are created, paragraphs and stanzas formatted, chapters built, and stories told. In a book or a poem, a play or a short story, everything is there, on the page, for a reason: To show, to tell, to convey a message. Most works of writing, quite simply, are meant for reading. The great ones, however, by the most talented and ingenious authors, are for study. In such works, it's the art one finds within that sets them apart from the rest.

Writers are influenced by the places in which they live and the cultures in which they are steeped. The writers in this volume lived during the late 1800s and early 1900s. Several individuals included in this volume, such as Oscar Wilde and George Eliot, are paradigms of English literature. Walt Whitman, Emily Dickinson, and Mark Twain are giants of American literature, while other authors featured here wrote in their native tongues in France, Russia, and Sweden. The Russian writer Leo Tolstoy was a novelist, essayist, and dramatist, and is most famous for his novel *War and Peace*, considered by many to be one of the greatest books ever put into print.

As the title of this book indicates, all those featured in this collection are influential writers. Through their work, they reached out to the masses, touched the hearts and souls of millions, and left their mark on the world. But how exactly is influence defined in this case? Perhaps it's the ability of one person, through his or her writing, to change the way the world thinks.

Perhaps a writer's influence is determined by timeless prominence, the ability to remain relevant hundreds of years after initial publication. All of the authors in this book fit that bill. This ability to sway audiences so deeply, and in so many ways, several centuries after the fact is arguably the very definition of influential.

With carefully crafted prose or a verse, a writer can influence individual allegiances, support or defame a political regime, or effect change by shedding light on an untenable situation. When all is said and done, perhaps what makes a writer influential is simply the ability to entertain, to keep readers up at night, turning page after page, just so they can learn what happens next.

The truth is, influence can mean so many things and can be measured in so many ways. Those who read the works of any of the writers profiled in this book may very well discover an experience they've perhaps never had before. They might have their imagination sparked and be transported, however briefly, from the travails of the life they're living. An author's writing might, with its insight, highlight an injustice, leading readers to speak out themselves and demand an equitable resolution. Whatever the case, one can't read a work by authors such as those detailed here without being influenced in some way. That's the power of great writing. And that's the real reason we read.

WALT WHITMAN

(b. May 31, 1819, West Hills, Long Island, N.Y., U.S.—d. March 26, 1892, Camden, N.J.)

Walt Whitman was an American poet, journalist, and essayist whose verse collection *Leaves of Grass* is a landmark in the history of American literature.

Whitman attended public school in Brooklyn, began working at the age of 12, and learned the printing trade. He was employed as a printer in Brooklyn and New York City, taught in country schools on Long Island, and became a journalist. At the age of 23 he edited a daily newspaper in New York, and in 1846 he became editor of the *Brooklyn Daily Eagle*, a fairly important newspaper of the time. Discharged from the *Eagle* early in 1848 because of his support for the Free Soil faction of the Democratic Party, he went to New Orleans, La., where he worked for three months on the *Crescent* before returning to New York via the Mississippi River and the Great Lakes. After another abortive attempt at Free Soil journalism, he built houses and dabbled in real estate in New York from about 1850 until 1855.

Whitman had spent a great deal of his 36 years walking and observing in New York City and Long Island. He had visited the theater frequently, and he had developed a strong love of music, especially opera. During these years he had also read extensively at home and in the New York libraries, and he began experimenting with a new style of poetry. While a schoolteacher, printer, and journalist he had published sentimental stories and poems in newspapers and popular magazines, but they showed almost no literary promise.

By the spring of 1855 Whitman had enough poems in his new style for a thin volume. Unable to find a publisher, he sold a house and printed the first edition of *Leaves of*

Grass at his own expense. No publisher's or author's name appeared on the first edition in 1855, but the cover had a portrait of Whitman. Though little appreciated upon its appearance, *Leaves of Grass* was warmly praised by the poet and essayist Ralph Waldo Emerson, who wrote to Whitman on receiving the poems that it was "the most extraordinary piece of wit and wisdom" America had yet contributed.

Whitman continued practicing his new style of writing in his private notebooks, and in 1856 the second edition of *Leaves of Grass* appeared. This collection contained revisions of the poems of the first edition and a new one, the *Sun-down Poem* (later to become *Crossing Brooklyn Ferry*). The second edition was also a financial failure, and once again Whitman edited a daily newspaper, the *Brooklyn Times*, but was unemployed by the summer of 1859. In 1860 a Boston publisher brought out the third edition of *Leaves of Grass*, greatly enlarged and rearranged, but the outbreak of the American Civil War bankrupted the firm.

During the Civil War, Whitman took a temporary post in the paymaster's office in Washington. He spent his spare time visiting wounded and dying soldiers in the Washington hospitals. In January 1865 he became a clerk in the Department of the Interior; in May he was promoted but in June was dismissed because the secretary of the Interior thought that *Leaves of Grass* was indecent. Whitman then obtained a post in the attorney general's office, largely through the efforts of his friend, the journalist William O'Connor, who wrote a vindication of Whitman.

In May 1865 a collection of war poems entitled *Drum Taps* showed Whitman's readers a new kind of poetry, moving from the oratorical excitement with which he had greeted the falling-in and arming of the young men at the beginning of the Civil War to a disturbing awareness of what war really meant. The *Sequel to Drum Taps*, published in the autumn of 1865, contained his great elegy on President Abraham Lincoln, *When Lilacs Last in the Dooryard Bloom'd*.

The fourth edition of *Leaves of Grass*, published in 1867, contained much revision and rearrangement, and in the late 1860s Whitman's work began to receive greater recognition. In January 1873 his first stroke left him partly paralyzed. Additional editions of *Leaves of Grass* followed, and the book finally reached the form in which it was henceforth to be published. *The Complete Poems and Prose* was published in 1888, along with the eighth edition of *Leaves of Grass*. The ninth, or "authorized," edition appeared in 1892, the year of Whitman's death.

Under the influence of the Romantic movement in literature and art, Whitman held the theory that the chief function of the poet was to express his own personality in his verse. The first edition of *Leaves of Grass* also appeared during the most nationalistic period in American literature, when critics were calling for a literature commensurate with the size, natural resources, and potentialities of the North American continent. From this time on throughout his life Whitman attempted to dress the part and act the role of the shaggy, untamed poetic spokesman of the proud young nation. For the expression of this persona he also created a form of free verse without rhyme or meter, but abounding in oratorical rhythms and chanted lists of American place-names and objects.

HERMAN MELVILLE

(b. Aug. 1, 1819, New York City—d. Sept. 28, 1891, New York City)

The American novelist, short-story writer, and poet Herman Melville is best known for his novels of the sea, including his masterpiece, *Moby Dick* (1851).

Born to a wealthy New York family that suffered great

financial losses, Melville had little formal schooling and began a period of wanderings at sea in 1839, when he served as cabin boy on a merchant ship. The summer voyage did not dedicate Melville to the sea. After a grinding search for work, he eventually sailed on the whaler *Acushnet*, from New Bedford, Mass., on a voyage to the South Seas.

In June 1842 the *Acushnet* anchored in present-day French Polynesia. Melville's adventures here, somewhat romanticized, became the subject of his first novel, *Typee* (1846). In July Melville and a companion jumped ship and, according to *Typee*, spent about four months as guest-captives of the reputedly cannibalistic Typee people. Actually, in August he was registered in the crew of the Australian whaler *Lucy Ann*. Whatever its precise correspondence with fact, however, *Typee* was faithful to the imaginative impact of the experience on Melville.

Although Melville was down for a 120th share of the whaler's proceeds, the voyage had been unproductive. He joined a mutiny that landed the mutineers in a Tahitian jail, from which he escaped without difficulty. On these events and their sequel, Melville based his second book, *Omoo* (1847). Lighthearted in tone, with the mutiny shown as something of a farce, it describes Melville's travels through the islands. In November he signed as a harpooner on his last whaler, the *Charles & Henry*, out of Nantucket, Mass. Six months later he disembarked at Lahaina, in the Hawaiian Islands. In August 1843 he signed as an ordinary seaman on the frigate *United States*, which in October 1844 discharged him in Boston.

Typee provoked immediate enthusiasm and outrage, and then a year later *Omoo* had an identical response. In 1847 Melville began a third book, *Mardi* (1849), and became a regular contributor of reviews and other pieces to a literary journal. When *Mardi* appeared, public and critics alike found its wild, allegorical fantasy and medley of styles incomprehensible. It began as another Polynesian adventure but quickly set its hero in pursuit of the mysterious Yillah, "all beauty and innocence," a symbolic quest that ends in anguish and disaster. Concealing his disappointment at the book's reception, Melville quickly wrote *Redburn* (1849) and *White-Jacket* (1850). The critics acclaimed *White-Jacket*, and its powerful criticism of abuses in the U.S. Navy won it strong political support. But both novels, however much they seemed to revive the Melville of *Typee*, had passages of profoundly questioning melancholy.

Melville had promised his publishers for the autumn of 1850 the novel first entitled *The Whale*, finally *Moby Dick*. His delay in submitting it was caused by his explorations into the unsuspected vistas opened for him by Nathaniel Hawthorne, whose *Scarlet Letter* he had read in the spring of 1850 and who became Melville's neighbor when Melville bought a farm near Hawthorne's home. Their relationship reanimated Melville's creative energies. On his side, it was dependent, almost mystically intense. To the cooler, withdrawn Hawthorne, such depth of feeling so persistently and openly declared was uncongenial. The two men gradually drew apart.

Moby Dick was published in London in October 1851 and a month later in America. It brought its author neither acclaim nor reward. Basically its story is simple. Captain Ahab pursues the white whale, Moby Dick, which finally kills him. At that level, it is an intense, superbly authentic narrative of whaling. In the perverted grandeur of Captain Ahab and in the beauties and terrors of the voyage of the *Pequod*, however, Melville dramatized his deeper concerns: the equivocal defeats and triumphs of the human spirit and its fusion of creative and murderous urges.

Increasingly a recluse, Melville embarked almost at once on *Pierre* (1852). It was an intensely personal work,

Herman Melville, etching after a portrait by Joseph O. Eaton. Library of Congress, Washington, D.C.

revealing the somber mythology of his private life framed in terms of a story of an artist alienated from his society. When published, it was another critical and financial disaster. Near breakdown, and having to face in 1853 the disaster of a fire at his New York publishers that destroyed most of his books, Melville persevered with writing. His contributions to *Putnam's Monthly Magazine*—"Bartleby the Scrivener" (1853), "The Encantadas" (1854), and "Benito Cereno" (1855)—reflected the despair and the contempt for human hypocrisy and materialism that possessed him increasingly. *The Confidence-Man* (1857), a despairing satire on an America corrupted by the shabby dreams of commerce, was the last of his novels to be published in his lifetime. Three American lecture tours were followed by his final sea journey, in 1860, when he joined his brother Thomas for a voyage around Cape Horn. He abandoned the trip in San Francisco. He then abandoned the novel for poetry for a time.

His return to prose culminated in his last work, the novel *Billy Budd*, which remained unpublished until 1924. Provoked by a false charge, the sailor Billy Budd accidentally kills the satanic master-at-arms. In a time of threatened mutiny he is hanged, going willingly to his fate. The manuscript ends with the date April 19, 1891. Five months later Melville died. By the end of the 1840s he was among the most celebrated of American writers, yet his death evoked but a single obituary notice.

GEORGE ELIOT

(b. Nov. 22, 1819, Chilvers Coton, Warwickshire, Eng.—d. Dec. 22, 1880, London)

George Eliot, the pseudonym of Mary Ann (or Marian) Evans, was an English Victorian novelist who developed the method of psychological analysis characteristic of modern fiction.

Evans had a strong evangelical piety instilled in her as a girl. In 1841 she moved with her father to Coventry, where she soon broke with her upbringing after she became acquainted with a prosperous ribbon manufacturer, Charles Bray, a self-taught freethinker who campaigned for radical causes.

In 1851 Evans moved to London to become a freelance writer, and, after a brief return to Coventry, she served for three years as subeditor of *The Westminster Review*, which under her influence enjoyed its most brilliant run since the days of John Stuart Mill. At evening parties in London she met many notable literary figures in an atmosphere of political and religious radicalism, including the subeditor of *The Economist*, Herbert Spencer, whose *Social Statics* (1851) had just been published. Evans shared many of Spencer's interests and saw so much of him that it was soon rumored that they were engaged. Though he did not become her husband, he introduced her to the two men who did.

One of those men was George Henry Lewes, a versatile Victorian journalist. In 1841 he had married Agnes Jervis, by whom he had four sons. But after two subsequent pregnancies by another man, Lewes ceased in 1851 to regard her as his wife. He had, however, condoned the adultery and was therefore precluded from suing for divorce. At this moment of dejection, his home hopelessly broken, he met Evans. They consulted about articles and went to plays and operas that Lewes reviewed for *The Leader*. Convinced that his break with Agnes was irrevocable, Evans determined to live openly with Lewes as his wife. In July 1854, after the publication of her translation of Feuerbach's *Essence of Christianity*, they went to Germany together. In all but the legal form it was a marriage, and it continued happily until Lewes's death in 1878.

At Weimar and Berlin, Evans wrote some of her best essays for *The Westminster* and translated Spinoza's *Ethics* (still unpublished), while Lewes worked on his groundbreaking life of Goethe. By his pen alone he had to support his three surviving sons at school in Switzerland as well as Agnes, whom he gave £100 a year, which was continued until her death in 1902. She turned to early memories and, encouraged by Lewes, wrote a story about a childhood episode in Chilvers Coton parish. Published in *Blackwood's Magazine* (1857) as *The Sad Fortunes of the Reverend Amos Barton*, it was an instant success. Two more tales, *Mr. Gilfil's Love-Story* and *Janet's Repentance*, also based on local events, appeared serially in the same year, and Blackwood republished all three as *Scenes of Clerical Life*, 2 vol. (1858) under the pseudonym George Eliot. It would become her pen name for the rest of her professional career.

Adam Bede, 3 vol. (1859), her first long novel, she described as "a country story—full of the breath of cows and the scent of hay." Its masterly realism brought to English fiction the same truthful observation of minute detail that Ruskin was commending in the Pre-Raphaelites. But what was new in this very popular novel was the combination of deep human sympathy and rigorous moral judgment. In *The Mill on the Floss*, 3 vol. (1860), Evans returned again to the scenes of her early life. The first half of the book, with its remarkable portrayal of childhood, is irresistibly appealing, and throughout there are scenes that reach a new level of psychological subtlety.

During their visit to Florence in 1860, Lewes suggested Savonarola as a good subject. Evans grasped it enthusiastically and began to plan *Romola* (1862–63). First, however, she wrote *Silas Marner* (1861). Its brevity and perfection of form made this story of the weaver whose lost gold is replaced by a strayed child the best known of her books. *Romola* was planned as a serial for *Blackwood's*, until an offer of £10,000 from *The Cornhill Magazine* induced Evans to desert her old publisher. Rather than divide the book into the 16 installments the editor wanted, she accepted £3,000 less, an evidence of artistic integrity few writers would have shown. It was published in 14 parts between July 1862 and August 1863.

Her next two novels are laid in England at the time of agitation for passage of the Reform Bill. In *Felix Holt, the Radical*, 3 vol. (1866), she drew the election riot from recollection of one she saw at Nuneaton in December 1832. *Middlemarch* (8 parts, 1871–72) is by general consent George Eliot's masterpiece. Every class of Middlemarch society is depicted from the landed gentry and clergy to the manufacturers and professional men, the shopkeepers, publicans, farmers, and laborers. Several strands of plot are interwoven to reinforce each other by contrast and parallel. Yet the story depends not on close-knit intrigue but on showing the incalculably diffusive effect of the unhistoric acts of anonymous individuals.

Daniel Deronda (8 parts, 1876) is built on the contrast between Mirah Cohen, a poor Jewish girl, and the upper class Gwendolen Harleth, who marries for money and regrets it. The hero, Daniel, after discovering that he is Jewish, marries Mirah and departs for Palestine to establish a home for his nation. The best part of *Daniel Deronda* is the keen analysis of Gwendolen's character, which seems to many critics the peak of George Eliot's achievement.

In 1863 the Leweses bought the Priory, 21, North Bank, Regent's Park, where their Sunday afternoons became a brilliant feature of Victorian life. There on Nov. 30, 1878, Lewes died. For nearly 25 years he had fostered Evans's genius and managed all the practical details of life, which now fell upon her. Most of all she missed the encouragement that alone made it possible for her to write. For some years her investments had been in the hands of John Walter Cross, a banker introduced to the Leweses by Herbert Spencer. On May 6, 1880, they were married. Cross was 40; she was in her 61st year. After a wedding trip in Italy they returned to her country house at Witley before moving to 4, Cheyne Walk, Chelsea, where she died in December. She was buried at Highgate Cemetery.

CHARLES BAUDELAIRE

(b. April 9, 1821, Paris, France—d. Aug. 31, 1867, Paris)

Charles Baudelaire was a French poet, translator, and literary and art critic whose reputation rests primarily on *Les Fleurs du mal* (1857; *The Flowers of Evil*), which was perhaps the most important and influential poetry collection published in Europe in the 19th century.

Regular acts of indiscipline led to his being expelled from the prestigious Lycée Louis-le-Grand after a trivial incident in April 1839. After passing his *baccalauréat* examinations while enrolled at the Collège Saint-Louis, Baudelaire became a nominal student of law at the École de Droit while in reality leading a "free life" in the Latin Quarter. There he made his first contacts in the literary world and also contracted the venereal disease that would eventually kill him, probably from a prostitute nicknamed Sarah la Louchette ("Squint-Eyed Sarah"), whom he celebrated in some of his most affecting early poems.

Baudelaire embarked on a protracted voyage to India in June 1841, but he effectively jumped ship in Mauritius and, after a few weeks there and in Réunion, returned to France in February 1842. He came into his inheritance in April 1842 and rapidly proceeded to dissipate it on the lifestyle of a dandified man of letters, spending freely on clothes, books, paintings, expensive food and wines, and, not least, hashish and opium. It was shortly after returning from the South Seas that Baudelaire met Jeanne Duval, who, first as his mistress and then, after the mid-1850s, as his financial charge, was to dominate his life for the next 20 years. Jeanne would inspire Baudelaire's most anguished and sensual love poetry, her perfume and, above all, her magnificent flowing black hair provoking such masterpieces of the exotic-erotic imagination as *La Chevelure* ("The Head of Hair"). Baudelaire's continuing extravagance exhausted half his fortune in two years, and he also fell prey to cheats and moneylenders, thus laying the foundation for an accumulation of debt that would cripple him for the rest of his life.

In 1847 Baudelaire discovered the work of Edgar Allan Poe. Overwhelmed by what he saw as the almost preternatural similarities between the American writer's thought and temperament and his own, he embarked upon the task of translation that was to provide him with his most regular occupation and income for the rest of his life. His translation of Poe's *Mesmeric Revelation* appeared as early as July 1848, and thereafter translations appeared regularly in reviews before being collected in book form in *Histoires extraordinaires* (1856; "Extraordinary Tales") and *Nouvelles Histoires extraordinaires* (1857; "New Extraordinary Tales"), each preceded by an important critical introduction by Baudelaire.

Baudelaire's growing reputation as Poe's translator and as an art critic at last enabled him to publish some of his poems. In June 1855 the *Revue des deux mondes* published a sequence of 18 of his poems under the general title of *Les Fleurs du mal*. The poems, which Baudelaire had chosen for their original style and startling themes, brought him notoriety. The following year Baudelaire signed a contract with the publisher Poulet-Malassis for a full-length poetry collection to appear with that title. When the first edition of *Les Fleurs du mal* was published in June 1857, 13 of its 100 poems were immediately arraigned for offences to religion or public morality. After a one-day trial on Aug. 20, 1857, six of the poems were ordered to be removed from the book on the grounds of obscenity, with Baudelaire incurring a fine of 300 (later reduced to 50) francs. The six poems were first republished in Belgium in 1866 in the collection *Les Épaves* ("Wreckage"), and the official ban on them would not be revoked until 1949. Owing largely to these circumstances, *Les Fleurs du mal* became a byword for depravity, morbidity, and obscenity, and the legend of Baudelaire as the doomed dissident and pornographic poet was born.

The failure of *Les Fleurs du mal*, from which he had expected so much, was a bitter blow to Baudelaire, and the remaining years of his life were darkened by a growing sense of despair. Although Baudelaire wrote some of his finest works in these years, few were published in book form. In 1859 Baudelaire produced in rapid succession a series of poetic masterpieces beginning with *Le Voyage* in January and culminating in what is widely regarded as his greatest single poem, *Le Cygne* ("The Swan"), in December. In February 1861 a second, and greatly enlarged and improved, edition of *Les Fleurs du mal* was published.

In 1861 Baudelaire made an ill-advised and unsuccessful attempt to gain election to the French Academy. Abandoning verse poetry as his medium, he now concentrated on writing prose poems, a sequence of 20 of which was published in *La Presse* in 1862. In 1864 he was stricken with paralysis and aphasia from which he would never recover. Baudelaire died at age 46 in the Paris nursing home in which he had been confined for the last year of his life.

At the time of Baudelaire's death, many of his writings were unpublished and those that had been published were

Charles Baudelaire (1821–1867) was primarily a poet, but he also published essays and his art and literary criticism were highly regarded.

out of print. This was soon to change, however. The future leaders of the Symbolist movement who attended his funeral were already describing themselves as his followers, and by the 20th century he was widely recognized as one of the greatest French poets of the 19th century.

FYODOR DOSTOYEVSKY

(b. Nov. 11, 1821, Moscow, Russia—d. Feb. 9, 1881, St. Petersburg)

Fyodor Mikhaylovich Dostoyevsky was a Russian novelist and short-story writer whose psychological penetration into the darkest recesses of the human heart, together with his unsurpassed moments of illumination, had an immense influence on 20th-century fiction.

Unlike many other Russian writers of the first part of the 19th century, Dostoyevsky was not born into the landed gentry. He often stressed the difference between his own background and that of Leo Tolstoy or Ivan Turgenev and the effect of that difference on his work. Dostoyevsky gave up a career as a military engineer (for which he was unsuited) in order to write.

In 1849 he was arrested for belonging to Petrashevsky Circle, a radical discussion group; sentenced to be shot, he was reprieved at the last moment. The mock-execution ceremony was in fact part of the punishment. One of the prisoners went permanently insane on the spot; another went on to write *Crime and Punishment*. Dostoyevsky was sentenced to four years in a Siberian prison labor camp, to be followed by an indefinite term as a soldier.

After his return to Russia 10 years later, he wrote a novel based on his prison camp experiences, *Zapiski iz myortvogo doma* (1861–62; *The House of the Dead*). Gone was the tinge of Romanticism and dreaminess present in his early fiction. The novel describes the horrors that Dostoyevsky actually witnessed: the brutality of the guards who enjoyed cruelty for its own sake, the evil of criminals who could enjoy murdering children, and the existence of decent souls amid filth and degradation—all these themes, warranted by the author's own experience, gave the novel the immense power that readers still experience.

In Siberia Dostoyevsky experienced what he called the "regeneration" of his convictions. He also suffered his first attacks of epilepsy. No less than his accounts of being led to execution, his descriptions of epileptic seizures (especially in *The Idiot*) reveal the heights and depths of the human soul. Later he published and wrote for several periodicals while producing his best novels. These novels are concerned especially with faith, suffering, and the meaning of life; they are famous for their psychological depth and insight and their near-prophetic treatment of issues in philosophy and politics. *Igrok* (1866; *The Gambler*) is based on his own gambling addiction. Among his best known is the novella *Zapiski iz podpolya* (1864; *Notes from the Underground*), in the first part of which an unnamed first-person narrator delivers a brilliant attack on a set of beliefs shared by liberals and radicals.

Then there are the great novels. *Prestupleniye i nakazaniye* (1866; *Crime and Punishment*) describes a young intellectual who is willing to gamble on ideas and decides to solve all his problems at a stroke by murdering an old pawnbroker woman. *Idiot* (1869; *The Idiot*) represents Dostoyevsky's attempt to describe a perfectly good man in a way that is still psychologically convincing, while *Besy* (1872; *The Possessed*) presents savage portraits of intellectuals but expresses great sympathy for workers and other ordinary people ill-served by the radicals who presume to speak in their name. *Bratya Karamazovy* (1879–80; *The Brothers Karamazov*) focuses on the problem of evil, the nature of freedom, and the craving for faith.

In 1876–77 Dostoyevsky devoted his energies to

Dnevnik pisatelya ("The Diary of a Writer"). A one-man journal, for which Dostoyevsky served as editor, publisher, and sole contributor, the *Diary* represented an attempt to initiate a new literary genre. Issue by monthly issue, it created complex thematic resonances among diverse kinds of material: short stories, plans for possible stories, autobiographical essays, sketches that seem to lie on the boundary between fiction and journalism, psychological analyses of sensational crimes, literary criticism, and political commentary. The *Diary* proved immensely popular and financially rewarding.

In 1880 Dostoyevsky delivered an electrifying speech about the poet Aleksandr Pushkin, which he published in a separate issue of *The Diary of a Writer* (August 1880). After finishing *Karamazov*, he resumed the monthly *Diary* but lived to publish only a single issue (January 1881) before dying of a hemorrhage on January 28 in St. Petersburg. By the end of his life, he had been acclaimed one of his country's greatest writers.

At least two modern literary genres, the prison camp novel and the dystopian novel (works such as Yevgeny Zamyatin's *We*, Aldous Huxley's *Brave New World*, and George Orwell's *1984*), derive from Dostoyevsky's writings. His ideas and formal innovations exercised a profound influence on Friedrich Nietzsche, André Gide, Albert Camus, and Jean-Paul Sartre, to name only a few. Above all, his works continue to enthrall readers by combining suspenseful plots with ultimate questions about faith, suffering, and the meaning of life.

GUSTAVE FLAUBERT

(b. Dec. 12, 1821, Rouen, France—d. May 8, 1880, Croisset)

The novelist Gustave Flaubert is regarded as the prime mover of the realist school of French literature and best known for his masterpiece, *Madame Bovary* (1857), a realistic portrayal of bourgeois life.

In 1841 Flaubert was enrolled as a student at the Faculty of Law in Paris. At age 22, however, he was recognized to be suffering from a nervous disease that was taken to be epilepsy. This made him give up the study of law, with the result that henceforth he could devote all his time to literature. Flaubert then retired to his estate at Croisset, near Rouen, on the Seine. He was to spend nearly all the rest of his life there.

The composition of *La Tentation de Saint Antoine* provides an example of that tenacity in the pursuit of perfection that made Flaubert go back constantly to work on subjects without ever being satisfied with the results. In 1839 he was writing *Smarh*, the first product of his bold ambition to give French literature its *Faust*. He resumed the task in 1846–49, in 1856, and in 1870, and finally published the book as *La Tentation de Saint Antoine* in 1874.

Madame Bovary was another work of long gestation. As early as 1837 he had written "Passion et vertu", a short and pointed story with a heroine, Mazza, resembling Emma Bovary. The novel itself cost the author five years of hard work prior to its appearance, with the subtitle *Moeurs de province* ("Provincial Customs"), in installments in the periodical *Revue* from October 1 to Dec. 15, 1856. For *Madame Bovary* he took a commonplace story of adultery and gave it an unrelenting objectivity—by which Flaubert meant the dispassionate recording of every trait or incident that could illuminate the psychology of his characters and their role in the logical development of his story—that transformed it into a work that represented the beginning of a new age in literature. The French government, however, brought the author to trial on the ground of his novel's alleged immorality, and he narrowly escaped conviction.

To refresh himself after his long application to the dull world of the bourgeoisie in *Madame Bovary*, Flaubert immediately began work on *Salammbô*, a novel about ancient Carthage. Subsequent works include *L'Éducation sentimentale* (1869), which appeared a few months before the outbreak of the Franco-German War of 1870 and was not appreciated by the public; several unsuccessful plays; and *Trois Contes* (1877), a book held to be his masterpiece that contains the three short stories "Un Coeur simple," "La Légende de Saint Julien l'Hospitalier," and "Hérodias." In the 1870s Flaubert sought consolation from financial troubles in his work and in the friendship of George Sand, Ivan Turgenev, and younger novelists—Émile Zola, Alphonse Daudet, and, especially, Guy de Maupassant. Flaubert's long novel *Bouvard et Pécuchet* was left unfinished when he died suddenly of an apoplectic stroke.

HENRIK IBSEN

(b. March 20, 1828, Skien, Nor.—d. May 23, 1906, Kristiania [formerly Christiania; now Oslo])

Henrik Ibsen was a major Norwegian playwright of the late 19th century who introduced to the European stage a new order of moral analysis that was placed against a severely realistic middle-class background and developed with economy of action, penetrating dialogue, and rigorous thought.

At the age of 23 Ibsen got himself appointed director and playwright to a new theater at Bergen, in which capacity he had to write a new play every year. First at Bergen and then at the Norwegian Theater in Christiania from 1857 to 1862, Ibsen tried to make palatable dramatic fare out of three incongruous ingredients: the drawing-room drama of the French playwright Eugène Scribe that was then popular; the actors, acting traditions, and language of Denmark; and the medieval Icelandic sagas—Norway's heroic, austere literature of unique magnificence. In addition to writing plays which were uncongenial to him and unacceptable to audiences, he did a lot of directing. In *Kongsemnerne* (1863; *The Pretenders*) he dramatized the mysterious inner authority that makes a man a man, a king, or a great playwright. This one play was in fact the national drama after which Ibsen had been groping so long, and before long it would be recognized as such.

The theater in Christiania soon went bankrupt, however. In April 1864 he left Norway for Italy. For the next 27 years he lived abroad, mainly in Rome, Dresden, and Munich, returning to Norway only for short visits in 1874 and 1885. For reasons that he sometimes summarized as "small-mindedness," his homeland had left a very bitter taste in his mouth.

With him into exile Ibsen brought the fragments of a long semi-dramatic poem to be named *Brand*. Its central figure is a dynamic rural pastor who takes his religious calling with a blazing sincerity that transcends not only all forms of compromise but all traces of human sympathy and warmth as well. In Norway *Brand* was a tremendous popular success, even though (and in part because) its central meaning was so troubling. Hard on the heels of *Brand* (1866) came *Peer Gynt* (1867), another drama in rhymed couplets presenting an utterly antithetical view of human nature. If Brand is a moral monolith, Peer Gynt is a capering will-o'-the-wisp, a buoyant and self-centered opportunist who is aimless, yielding, and wholly unprincipled, yet who remains a lovable and beloved rascal.

With these two poetic dramas, Ibsen won his battle with the world; he paused now to work out his future. But Ibsen had not yet found his proper voice. When he did, its effect was not to criticize or reform social life but to blow it up. The explosion came with *Et dukkehjem* (1879; *A Doll's House*), about a very ordinary family that disintegrates. Audiences were scandalized at Ibsen's refusal in *A Doll's House* to scrape together (as any other contemporary playwright would have done) a "happy ending," however shoddy or contrived. But that was not Ibsen's way; his play was about knowing oneself and being true to that self.

Ibsen's next play, *Gengangere* (1881; *Ghosts*), created even more dismay and distaste than its predecessor by showing worse consequences of covering up even more ugly truths. Ostensibly the play's theme is congenital venereal disease, but on another level, it deals with the power of ingrained moral contamination to undermine the most determined idealism. The play is a grim study of contamination spreading through a family under cover of the widowed Mrs. Alving's timidly respectable views.

Among his later plays are *Fruen fra havet* (1888; *The Lady from the Sea*), *Hedda Gabler* (1890), *Bygmester Solness* (1892; *The Master Builder*), *Lille Eyolf* (1894; *Little Eyolf*), and *Naar vi døde vaagner* (1899; *When We Dead Awaken*). Two of these plays, *Hedda Gabler* and *The Master Builder*, are vitalized by the presence of a demonically idealistic and totally destructive female. Another obsessive personage in these late plays is an aging artist who is bitterly aware of his failing powers. Personal and confessional feelings infuse many of these last dramas; perhaps these resulted from Ibsen's decision in 1891 to return to Norway, or perhaps from the series of fascinated, fearful dalliances he had with young women in his later years. After his return to Norway, Ibsen continued to write plays until a stroke in 1900 and another a year later reduced him to a bedridden invalid. He died in Kristiania in 1906.

LEO TOLSTOY

(b. Aug. 28 [Sept. 9, New Style], 1828, Yasnaya Polyana, Tula province, Russian Empire—d. Nov. 7 [Nov. 20], 1910, Astapovo, Ryazan province)

Leo Tolstoy, the Russian master of realistic fiction, is one of the world's greatest novelists. The scion of prominent aristocrats, Tolstoy spent much of his life at his family estate of Yasnaya Polyana. Educated at home by tutors, Tolstoy enrolled in the University of Kazan in 1844. His poor record soon forced him to transfer to the less demanding law faculty, where he began to pursue his interests in literature and ethics. He left the university in 1847 without a degree. He served in the army, which included service in the Crimean War (1853–56).

Among his early published works are three sketches about the Siege of Sevastopol: "Sevastopol v dekabre mesyatse" ("Sevastopol in December"), "Sevastopol v maye" ("Sevastopol in May"), and "Sevastopol v avguste 1855 goda" ("Sevastopol in August"; all published 1855–56). Tolstoy was at first hailed by the literary world of St. Petersburg. But his prickly vanity, his refusal to join any intellectual camp, and his insistence on his complete independence soon earned him the dislike of the radical intelligentsia. He was to remain throughout his life an "archaist," opposed to prevailing intellectual trends.

He traveled in Europe before returning home and starting a school for peasant children. His novel *Kazaki* (1863; *The Cossacks*) was among the works from a period during which he experimented with new forms for expressing his moral and philosophical concerns. *Voyna i mir* (1865–69; *War and Peace*) marked the beginning of the period during which Tolstoy reached the height of his creative powers. It contains three kinds of material—a historical account of the Napoleonic wars, the biographies of fictional characters, and a set of essays about the philosophy of history. It examines the lives of a large group of characters, centering on the partly autobiographical figure of the spiritually questing Pierre. Its structure, with its flawless placement of complex characters in a turbulent historical setting, is regarded as one of the great technical achievements in the history of the Western novel.

His other great novel, *Anna Karenina* (1875–77), takes family life as its concern. The novel's first sentence, which indicates its concern with the domestic, is perhaps Tolstoy's most famous: "All happy families resemble each other; each unhappy family is unhappy in its own way." Both *War and Peace* and *Anna Karenina* advance the idea that ethics can never be a matter of timeless rules applied to particular situations. Rather, ethics depends on a sensitivity, developed over a lifetime, to particular people and specific situations. Tolstoy's preference for particularities over abstractions is often described as the hallmark of his thought.

After the publication of *Anna Karenina* Tolstoy underwent a spiritual crisis (described in *Ispoved*, 1884; *My Confession*). Drawn at first to the Russian Orthodox church into which he had been born, he rapidly decided that it, and all other Christian churches, were corrupt institutions that had thoroughly falsified true Christianity. Having discovered what he believed to be Christ's message and having overcome his paralyzing fear of death, Tolstoy devoted the rest of his life to developing and propagating his new faith, which stressed simplicity, nonviolence, and social reform. He was excommunicated from the Russian Orthodox church in 1901.

Among his later works is *Smert Ivana Ilicha* (written 1886; *The Death of Ivan Ilyich*), a novella describing a man's gradual realization that he is dying and that his life has been wasted on trivialities; it is often considered the greatest novella in Russian literature. Tolstoy also wrote a treatise and several essays on art. In *Chto takoye iskusstvo?* (1898; *What Is Art?*), for instance, he argued that true art requires a sensitive appreciation of a particular experience, a highly specific feeling that is communicated to the reader not by propositions but by "infection."

Tolstoy lived humbly on his great estate, practicing a radical asceticism and in constant conflict with his wife. In November 1910, unable to bear his situation any longer, he left his estate incognito, although the international press was soon able to report on his movements. During his flight he contracted pneumonia, and died of heart failure at the railroad station of Astapovo.

EMILY DICKINSON

(b. Dec. 10, 1830, Amherst, Mass., U.S.—d. May 15, 1886, Amherst)

The American lyric poet Emily Dickinson, who lived in seclusion and commanded a singular brilliance of style and integrity of vision, is widely considered to be one of the leading 19th-century American poets.

Early Years

The second of three children, Dickinson grew up in moderate privilege and with strong local and religious attachments. For her first nine years she resided in a mansion built by her paternal grandfather, Samuel Fowler Dickinson, who had helped found Amherst College but then went bankrupt shortly before her birth. Her parents were loving but austere, and she became closely attached to her brother, Austin, and sister, Lavinia. Never marrying, the two sisters remained at home, and when their brother married, he and his wife established their own household next door.

Dickinson attended the coeducational Amherst Academy, where she was recognized by teachers and students alike for her prodigious abilities in composition. She also excelled in other subjects emphasized by the school, most notably Latin and the sciences. When she left home to attend Mount Holyoke Female Seminary (now Mount Holyoke College) in nearby South Hadley, she found the school's institutional tone uncongenial. Mount Holyoke's strict rules and invasive religious practices, along with her own homesickness and growing rebelliousness, help explain why she did not return for a second year.

At home as well as at school and church, the religious faith that ruled the poet's early years was evangelical Calvinism, a faith centered on the belief that humans are born totally depraved and can be saved only if they undergo a life-altering conversion in which they accept the vicarious sacrifice of Jesus Christ. Questioning this tradition soon after leaving Mount Holyoke, Dickinson was to be the only member of her family who did not experience conversion or join Amherst's First Congregational Church. Yet she seems to have retained a belief in the soul's immortality or at least to have transmuted it into a Romantic quest for the transcendent and absolute. One reason her mature religious views elude specification is that she took no interest in creedal or doctrinal definition. In this she was influenced by both the Transcendentalism of Ralph Waldo Emerson and the mid-century tendencies of liberal Protestant orthodoxy.

Development as a Poet

Although Dickinson had begun composing verse by her

late teens, few of her early poems are extant. Until she was in her mid-20s, her writing mostly took the form of letters, and a surprising number of those that she wrote from age 11 onward have been preserved. Sent to her brother, Austin, or to friends of her own sex, especially Abiah Root, Jane Humphrey, and Susan Gilbert (who would marry Austin), these generous communications overflow with humor, anecdote, invention, and somber reflection. In general, Dickinson seems to have given and demanded more from her correspondents than she received. On occasion she interpreted her correspondents' laxity in replying as evidence of neglect or even betrayal. Indeed, the loss of friends, whether through death or cooling interest, became a basic pattern for Dickinson. Much of her writing, both poetic and epistolary, seems premised on a feeling of abandonment and a matching effort to deny, overcome, or reflect on a sense of solitude.

Dickinson's closest friendships usually had a literary flavor. She was introduced to the poetry of Ralph Waldo Emerson by one of her father's law students, Benjamin F. Newton, and to that of Elizabeth Barrett Browning by Susan Gilbert and Henry Vaughan Emmons, a gifted college student. Two of Barrett Browning's works, *A Vision of Poets*, describing the pantheon of poets, and *Aurora Leigh*, on the development of a female poet, seem to have played a formative role for Dickinson, validating the idea of female greatness and stimulating her ambition.

In 1855 Dickinson traveled to Washington, D.C., with her sister and father, who was then ending his term as U.S. representative. On the return trip the sisters made an extended stay in Philadelphia, where it is thought the poet heard the preaching of Charles Wadsworth, a fascinating Presbyterian minister whose pulpit oratory suggested (as a colleague put it) "years of conflict and agony." Seventy years later, Martha Dickinson Bianchi, the poet's niece, claimed that Emily had fallen in love with Wadsworth, who was married, and then grandly renounced him. The story is too highly colored for its details to be credited; certainly, there is no evidence the minister returned the poet's love. Yet it is true that a correspondence arose between the two and that Wadsworth visited her in Amherst about 1860, and again in 1880.

Always fastidious, Dickinson began to restrict her social activity in her early 20s, staying home from communal functions and cultivating intense epistolary relationships with a reduced number of correspondents. In 1855, leaving the large and much-loved house in which she had lived for 15 years, the 25-year-old woman and her family moved back to the dwelling associated with her first decade: the Dickinson mansion on Main Street in Amherst. She found the return profoundly disturbing, and when her mother became incapacitated by a mysterious illness that lasted from 1855 to 1859, both daughters were compelled to give more of themselves to domestic pursuits.

Mature Career

In summer 1858, Dickinson began assembling her manuscript-books. She made clean copies of her poems on fine quality stationery and then sewed small bundles of these sheets together at the fold. Over the next seven years she created 40 such booklets and several unsewn sheaves, and altogether they contained about 800 poems.

Dickinson sent more poems to her sister-in-law, Susan Gilbert Dickinson, a cultivated reader, than to any other known correspondent. Repeatedly professing eternal allegiance, these poems often imply that there was a certain distance between the two—that the sister-in-law was felt to be haughty, remote, or even incomprehensible. Yet Susan admired the poetry's wit and verve and offered the kind of personally attentive audience Dickinson craved. Susan was an active hostess, and her home was the venue at which Dickinson met a few friends, most importantly Samuel Bowles, publisher and editor of the influential *Springfield Republican*. Gregarious, captivating, and unusually liberal on the question of women's careers, Bowles had a high regard for Dickinson's poems, publishing (without her consent) seven of them during her lifetime—more than appeared in any other outlet.

In those years Dickinson experienced a painful and obscure personal crisis, partly of a romantic nature. The abject and pleading drafts of her second and third letters to the unidentified person she called "Master" are probably related to her many poems about a loved but distant person, usually male. Whoever the person was, Master's failure to return Dickinson's affection—together with Susan's absorption in her first childbirth and Bowles's growing invalidism—contributed to a piercing and ultimate sense of distress. Instead of succumbing to anguish, however, she came to view it as the sign of a special vocation, and it became the basis of an unprecedented creativity.

In April 1862, about the time Wadsworth left the East Coast for a pastorate in San Francisco, Dickinson sought the critical advice of Thomas Wentworth Higginson, whose witty article of advice to writers, *A Letter to a Young Contributor*, had just appeared in *The Atlantic Monthly*. Higginson was known as a writer of delicate nature essays and a crusader for women's rights. Enclosing four poems, Dickinson asked for his opinion of her verse—whether or not it was "alive." The ensuing correspondence lasted for years, with the poet sending her "preceptor," as she called him, many more samples of her work. In addition to seeking an informed critique from a professional but not unsympathetic man of letters, she was reaching out at a time of accentuated loneliness.

Dickinson's last trips from Amherst were in 1864 and 1865, when she shared her cousins Louisa and Frances Norcross's boardinghouse in Cambridge and underwent a course of treatment with the leading Boston ophthalmologist. She described her symptoms as an aching in her eyes and a painful sensitivity to light. In 1869 Higginson invited the poet to Boston to attend a literary salon; she refused the offer. When Higginson visited her the next year, he recorded his vivid first impression of her "plain" features, "exquisitely" neat attire, "childlike" manner, and loquacious and exhausting brilliance. He was "glad not to live near her."

In her last 15 years Dickinson averaged 35 poems a year and conducted her social life mainly through her chiselled and often sibylline written messages. Her father's sudden death in 1874 caused a profound and persisting emotional upheaval yet eventually led to a greater openness, self-possession, and serenity. She repaired an 11-year breach with Samuel Bowles and made friends with Maria Whitney, a teacher of modern languages at Smith College, and Helen Hunt Jackson, poet and author of the novel *Ramona* (1884). Dickinson resumed contact with Wadsworth, and from about age 50 she conducted a passionate romance with Otis Phillips Lord, an elderly judge on the supreme court of Massachusetts. The letters she apparently sent Lord reveal her at her most playful, alternately teasing and confiding. In declining an erotic advance or his proposal of marriage, she asked, "Dont you know you are happiest while I withhold and not confer—dont you know that 'No' is the wildest word we consign to Language?"

After Dickinson's aging mother was incapacitated by a stroke and a broken hip, caring for her at home made large demands on the poet's time and patience. The deaths of Dickinson's friends in her last years left her feeling terminally alone. But the single most shattering death, occurring in 1883, was that of her eight-year-old nephew next door. Her health broken by this culminating tragedy, she ceased seeing almost everyone, apparently including her sister-in-law. The poet died in 1886, when she was 55 years old. The immediate cause of death was a stroke.

Only 10 of Emily Dickinson's nearly 1,800 poems are known to have been published in her lifetime. She habitually worked in verse forms suggestive of hymns and ballads, with lines of three or four stresses. Her unusual off-rhymes have been seen as both experimental and influenced by the 18th-century hymnist Isaac Watts. She freely ignored the usual rules of versification and even of grammar, and in the intellectual content of her work she likewise proved exceptionally bold and original. Her verse is distinguished by its epigrammatic compression, haunting personal voice, enigmatic brilliance, and lack of high polish.

LEWIS CARROLL

(b. Jan. 27, 1832, Daresbury, Cheshire, Eng.—d. Jan. 14, 1898, Guildford, Surrey)

Lewis Carroll, the pseudonym of Charles Lutwidge Dodgson, was a English logician, mathematician, photographer, and novelist who is especially remembered for *Alice's Adventures in Wonderland* (1865) and its sequel, *Through the Looking-Glass* (1871).

Dodgson excelled in his mathematical and classical studies at the Christ Church, Oxford, which he entered as an undergraduate in 1851; he proceeded to a Bachelor of Arts degree in 1854. He was made a "senior student" (called a fellow in other colleges) and appointed lecturer in mathematics in 1855, a post he resigned in 1881. As was the case with all fellowships at that time, the studentship was dependent upon his remaining unmarried, and, by the terms of this particular endowment, proceeding to holy orders. Dodgson was ordained a deacon in the Church of England on Dec. 22, 1861. Had he gone on to become a priest he could have married and would then have been appointed to a parish by the college. But he felt himself unsuited for parish work and decided that he was perfectly content to remain a bachelor.

Dodgson's association with children grew naturally enough out of his position as an eldest son with eight younger brothers and sisters. He also suffered from a bad stammer (which he never wholly overcame) and found that he was able to speak naturally and easily to children. It is therefore not surprising that he should begin to entertain the children of Henry George Liddell, dean of Christ Church. Alice Liddell and her sisters Lorina and Edith were not the first of Dodgson's child friends. They had been preceded or were overlapped by the children of the writer George Macdonald, the sons of the poet Alfred, Lord Tennyson, and various other chance acquaintances. But the Liddell children undoubtedly held an especially high place in his affections—partly because they were the only children in Christ Church, since only heads of houses were free both to marry and to continue in residence.

On July 4, 1862, Dodgson and his friend Robinson Duckworth, fellow of Trinity, rowed the three children up the Thames from Oxford to Godstow, picnicked on the bank, and returned to Christ Church late in the evening: "On which occasion," wrote Dodgson in his diary, "I told them the fairy-tale of *Alice's Adventures Underground*, which I undertook to write out for Alice." Much of the story was based on a picnic a couple of weeks earlier when they had all been caught in the rain; for some reason, this inspired Dodgson to tell so much better a story than usual that both Duckworth and Alice noticed the difference, and Alice went so far as to cry, when they parted at the door of the deanery, "Oh, Mr. Dodgson, I wish you would write out Alice's adventures for me!"

Dodgson was able to write down the story more or less as told and added to it several extra adventures that had been told on other occasions. He illustrated it with his own crude but distinctive drawings and gave the finished product to Alice Liddell, with no thought of hearing of it again. But the novelist Henry Kingsley, while visiting the deanery, chanced to pick it up from the drawing-room table, read it, and urged Mrs. Liddell to persuade the author to publish it. Dodgson, honestly surprised, consulted his friend George Macdonald, author of some of the best children's stories of the period. Macdonald took it home to be read to his children, and his son Greville, aged six, declared that he "wished there were 60,000 volumes of it."

Accordingly, Dodgson revised it for publication. At Duckworth's suggestion he got an introduction to John Tenniel, the *Punch* magazine cartoonist, whom he commissioned to make illustrations to his specification. The book was published as *Alice's Adventures in Wonderland* in 1865.The book was a slow but steadily increasing success, and by the following year Dodgson was already considering a sequel to it. The result was *Through the Looking-Glass and What Alice Found There* (dated 1872; actually published December 1871). By the time of Dodgson's death, *Alice* (taking the two volumes as a single artistic triumph) had become the most popular children's book in England: by the time of his centenary in 1932 it was one of the most popular and perhaps the most famous in the world.

Before he had told the original tale of *Alice's Adventures*, Dodgson had published a number of humorous items in verse and prose and a few inferior serious poems. The earliest of these appeared anonymously, but in March 1856 a poem called *Solitude* was published under the pseudonym Lewis Carroll. Dodgson arrived at this pen name by taking his own names Charles Lutwidge, translating them into Latin as Carolus Ludovicus, then reversing and retranslating them into English. He used the name afterward for all his nonacademic works. His humorous and other verses were collected in 1869 as *Phantasmagoria and Other Poems* and later separated (with additions) as *Rhyme? and Reason?* (1883) and *Three Sunsets and Other Poems* (published posthumously, 1898). The 1883 volume also contained *The Hunting of the Snark*, a narrative nonsense poem that is rivalled only by the best of Edward Lear.

MARK TWAIN

(b. Nov. 30, 1835, Florida, Mo., U.S.—d. April 21, 1910, Redding, Conn.)

Mark Twain (the pseudonym of Samuel Clemens) was an American humorist, journalist, lecturer, and novelist who acquired international fame for his travel narratives, especially *The Innocents Abroad* (1869), *Roughing It* (1872), and *Life on the Mississippi* (1883), and for his adventure stories of boyhood, especially *The Adventures of Tom Sawyer* (1876) and *Adventures of Huckleberry Finn* (1885). A gifted raconteur, distinctive humorist, and irascible moralist, he transcended the apparent limitations of his origins to become a popular public figure and one of America's best and most beloved writers.

Youth and Apprenticeships

Samuel Clemens, the sixth child of John Marshall and Jane Moffit Clemens, was born two months prematurely and was in relatively poor health for the first 10 years of his life. It was the diminishing fortunes of the Clemens family that led them in 1839 to move 30 miles (50 km) east from Florida, Mo., to the Mississippi River port town of Hannibal, where there were greater opportunities. John

Clemens opened a store and eventually became a justice of the peace, which entitled him to be called "Judge" but not to a great deal more.

In 1848 Clemens became a printer's apprentice for Joseph P. Ament's *Missouri Courier*. He lived sparingly in the Ament household but was allowed to continue his schooling and, from time to time, indulge in boyish amusements. Nevertheless, by the time Clemens was 13, his boyhood had effectively come to an end. He became more than competent as a typesetter while working for his brother, who owned a newspaper, but he also occasionally contributed sketches and articles. Some of those early sketches, such as *The Dandy Frightening the Squatter* (1852), appeared in Eastern newspapers and periodicals.

Having acquired a trade by age 17, Clemens left Hannibal in 1853 with some degree of self-sufficiency. For almost two decades he would be an itinerant laborer, trying many occupations. It was not until he was 37, he once remarked, that he woke up to discover he had become a "literary person." In the meantime, he was intent on seeing the world and exploring his own possibilities. He worked briefly as a typesetter in St. Louis in 1853 before working in New York City, Philadelphia, and Washington, D.C. He continued to write, though without firm literary ambitions.

Still restless and ambitious, he booked passage in 1857 on a steamboat bound for New Orleans, La., planning to find his fortune in South America. Instead, he saw a more immediate opportunity and persuaded the accomplished riverboat captain Horace Bixby to take him on as an apprentice. Clemens studied the Mississippi River and the operation of a riverboat under the masterful instruction of Bixby, with an eye toward obtaining a pilot's license, which he did in 1859. The profession of riverboat pilot was, as he confessed many years later in *Old Times on the*

Mississippi, the most congenial one he had ever followed. He continued to write occasional pieces throughout these years and, in one satirical sketch, *River Intelligence* (1859), lampooned the self-important senior pilot Isaiah Sellers, whose observations of the Mississippi were published in a New Orleans newspaper. Clemens and the other "starchy boys," as he once described his fellow riverboat pilots in a letter to his wife, had no particular use for this nonunion man, but Clemens did envy what he later recalled to be Sellers's delicious pen name, Mark Twain.

The Civil War severely curtailed river traffic, and, fearing that he might be pressed into service as a Union gunboat pilot, Clemens brought his years on the river to a halt in 1861. After a sojourn in Hannibal, Clemens accompanied his brother Orion to the Nevada Territory, where Sam had to shift for himself. He submitted several letters to the Virginia City *Territorial Enterprise*, and these attracted the attention of the editor, Joseph Goodman, who offered him a salaried job as a reporter. He again embarked on an apprenticeship, in the hearty company of a group of writers sometimes called the Sagebrush Bohemians, and again he succeeded.

In February 1863 Clemens covered the legislative session in Carson City and wrote three letters for the *Enterprise*. He signed them "Mark Twain." Apparently the mistranscription of a telegram misled Clemens to believe that the pilot Isaiah Sellers had died and that his cognomen was up for grabs. Clemens seized it. It would be several years before this pen name would acquire the firmness of a full-fledged literary persona, however. In the meantime, he was discovering by degrees what it meant to be a "literary person." Some of his articles and sketches had appeared in New York papers, and he became the Nevada correspondent for the San Francisco *Morning Call*. A period as a reporter in San Francisco followed.

He then went to the Tuolumne foothills to do some mining. It was there that he heard the story of a jumping frog. The story was widely known, but it was new to Clemens, and he took notes for a literary representation of the tale. When the humorist Artemus Ward invited him to contribute something for a book of humorous sketches, Clemens decided to write up the story. *Jim Smiley and His Jumping Frog* arrived too late to be included in the volume, but it was published in the New York *Saturday Press* in November 1865 and was subsequently reprinted throughout the country. "Mark Twain" had acquired sudden celebrity, and Sam Clemens was following in his wake.

LITERARY MATURITY

The next few years were important for Clemens. It appears that he was committed to making a professional career for himself. He continued to write for newspapers, traveling to Hawaii for the Sacramento *Union* and also writing for New York newspapers, but he apparently wanted to become something more than a journalist. He went on his first lecture tour, speaking mostly on the Sandwich Islands (Hawaii) in 1866. It was a success, and for the rest of his life, though he found touring grueling, he knew he could take to the lecture platform when he needed money. His first book was *The Celebrated Jumping Frog of Calaveras County and Other Sketches* (1867), but it did not sell well. That same year, he moved to New York City, serving as the traveling correspondent for the San Francisco *Alta California* and for New York newspapers. He had ambitions to enlarge his reputation and his audience, and the announcement of a transatlantic excursion to Europe and the Holy Land provided him with just such an opportunity. The *Alta* paid the substantial fare in exchange for some 50 letters he would write concerning the trip.

Eventually his account of the voyage was published as *The Innocents Abroad* (1869). It was a great success.

The trip abroad was fortuitous in another way. He met on the boat a young man named Charlie Langdon, who invited Clemens to dine with his family in New York and introduced him to his sister Olivia; the writer fell in love with her. Clemens's courtship of Olivia Langdon, the daughter of a prosperous businessman from Elmira, N.Y., was an ardent one, conducted mostly through correspondence. They were married in February 1870.

A book about his experiences in the West, *Roughing It*, was published in February 1872 and sold well. *The Gilded Age* (1873), Twain's first attempt at a novel, was remarkably well received and encouraged him to begin writing *Tom Sawyer*, along with his reminiscences about his days as a riverboat pilot. The latter became *Old Times*, which in turn would later become a portion of *Life on the Mississippi*. It described comically, but a bit ruefully too, a way of life that would never return. The highly episodic narrative of *Tom Sawyer* (1876), which recounts the mischievous adventures of a boy growing up along the Mississippi River, was colored by a nostalgia for childhood and simplicity that would permit Twain to characterize the novel as a "hymn" to childhood.

In the summer of 1876, while staying with his in-laws Susan and Theodore Crane on Quarry Farm overlooking Elmira, Clemens began writing what he called in a letter to his friend William Dean Howells "Huck Finn's Autobiography." Huck had appeared as a character in *Tom Sawyer*, and Clemens decided that the untutored boy had his own story to tell. He soon discovered that it had to be told in Huck's own vernacular voice. *Huckleberry Finn* was written in fits and starts over an extended period and would not be published until 1885. During that interval, Twain often turned his attention to other projects, only to return again and again to the novel's manuscript. What distinguishes *Huckleberry Finn* from the other Huck-and-Tom sequels that Twain wrote is the moral dilemma Huck faces in aiding the runaway slave Jim while at the same time escaping from the unwanted influences of so-called civilization. Through Huck, the novel's narrator, Twain was able to address the shameful legacy of chattel slavery prior to the Civil War and the persistent racial discrimination and violence after.

Clemens's travels at home and abroad resulted in several books published during the 1880s. He embarked on a lecture tour in 1884. All the while, however, he continued to make often ill-advised investments. Clemens eventually assigned his property, including his copyrights, to his wife, announced the failure of his publishing house, and declared personal bankruptcy. In 1894, approaching his 60th year, Samuel Clemens was forced to repair his fortunes and remake his career.

Old Age

Clemens's last years have been described as his "bad mood" period. The description may or may not be apt. His eldest daughter died in 1896, his wife in 1904, and another daughter in 1909. It is true that in his polemical essays and in much of his fiction during this time he was venting powerful moral feelings and commenting freely on the "damn'd human race." But he had always been against sham and corruption, greed, cruelty, and violence. Some of Twain's best work during his late years was not fiction but polemical essays in which his earnestness was not in doubt: an essay against anti-Semitism, *Concerning the Jews* (1899); a denunciation of imperialism, *To the Man Sitting in Darkness* (1901); and an essay on lynching, *The United States of Lyncherdom* (posthumously published in 1923). Yet this was also a period during which he received palpable tokens of public approbation in the form of three honorary degrees—from Yale University in 1901, from the University of Missouri in 1902, and, the one he most coveted, from Oxford University in 1907.

More important, a world lecture tour and the publication of *Following the Equator* (1897), which described that tour, combined with shrewd investments of his money, allowed Clemens to pay his creditors in full. He traveled to Bermuda in January 1910. By early April he was having severe chest pains, and he returned to his home in Connecticut, where he died.

ÉMILE ZOLA

(b. April 2, 1840, Paris, France—d. Sept. 28, 1902, Paris)

Émile Zola, a French critic and political activist, was also the most prominent French novelist of the late 19th century. Raised in straitened circumstances, Zola worked at a Paris publishing house and as a journalist during the 1860s while establishing himself as a fiction writer. Two early novels are *Thérèse Raquin* (1867), a grisly tale of murder and its aftermath, and *Madeleine Férat* (1868), a rather unsuccessful attempt at applying the principles of heredity to the novel.

It was this interest in science that led Zola, in the fall of 1868, to conceive the idea of a large-scale series of novels similar to Honoré de Balzac's *La Comédie humaine* (*The Human Comedy*), which had appeared earlier in the century. Zola's project, originally involving 10 novels, each featuring a different member of the same family, was gradually expanded to comprise the 20 volumes of the *Rougon-Macquart* series. *La Fortune des Rougon* (*The Rougon Family Fortune*), the first novel in the series, began to appear in serial form in 1870, was interrupted by the outbreak of the Franco-German War in July, and was eventually published in book form in October 1871. Zola went on to produce these 20 novels—most of which are of substantial length—at the rate of nearly one per year, completing the series in 1893. The series thus constitutes a family saga while providing a valuable sociological document of the events, institutions, and ideas that marked the rise of modern industrialism and the cultural changes it entailed.

As the founder and most celebrated member of the naturalist movement, Zola also published several treatises to explain his theories on art, including *Le Roman expérimental* (1880; *The Experimental Novel*) and *Les Romanciers naturalistes* (1881; *The Naturalist Novelists*). Naturalism, as Zola explained, involves the application to literature of two scientific principles: determinism, or the belief that character, temperament, and, ultimately, behavior are determined by the forces of heredity, environment, and historical moment; and the experimental method, which entails the objective recording of precise data in controlled conditions.

In 1898 Zola intervened in the Dreyfus Affair—that of a Jewish French army officer whose wrongful conviction for treason in 1894 sparked a 12-year controversy that deeply divided French society. At an early stage in the proceedings Zola had decided, rightly, that Alfred Dreyfus was innocent. On Jan. 13, 1898, in the newspaper *L'Aurore*, Zola published a fierce denunciation of the French general staff in an open letter beginning with the words "J'accuse" ("I accuse"). He charged various high-ranking military officers and, indeed, the War Office itself of concealing the truth in the wrongful conviction of Dreyfus for espionage. Zola was prosecuted for libel and found guilty. In July 1899, when his appeal appeared certain to fail, he fled to England. He returned to France the following June when he learned that the Dreyfus case was to be reopened with a possible reversal of the original verdict. Zola's intervention in the controversy helped to undermine anti-Semitism and rabid militarism in France.

Zola died unexpectedly in September 1902, the victim of coal gas asphyxiation resulting from a blocked chimney flue. He had produced some 60 volumes of fiction, theory, and criticism, in addition to numerous pieces of journalism, during his 40-year career. At the time of his death, Zola was recognized not only as one of the greatest novelists in Europe but also as a man of action—a defender of truth and justice, a champion of the poor and the persecuted.

HENRY JAMES

(b. April 15, 1843, New York, N.Y., U.S.—d. Feb. 28, 1916, London, Eng.)

Henry James was an American novelist and, as a naturalized English citizen, a great figure in the transatlantic culture. His fundamental theme was the innocence and exuberance of the New World in clash with the corruption and wisdom of the Old.

He was named for his father, a prominent social theorist and lecturer, and was the younger brother of the pragmatist philosopher William James. They were taken abroad as infants, were schooled by tutors and governesses, and spent their preadolescent years in Manhattan. Returned to Geneva, Paris, and London during their teens, the James children acquired languages and an awareness of Europe few Americans had in their times. When he was 19 years of age Henry enrolled at the Harvard Law School, but he devoted his study time to reading Charles-Augustin Sainte-Beuve, Honoré de Balzac, and Nathaniel Hawthorne. His first story appeared anonymously two years later in the New York *Continental*

Monthly and his first book reviews in the *North American Review*. By his mid-20s James was regarded as one of the most skillful writers of short stories in America.

James began his long expatriation in the 1870s, heralded by publication of the novel *Roderick Hudson* (1875), the story of an American sculptor's struggle by the banks of the Tiber between his art and his passions; *Transatlantic Sketches*, his first collection of travel writings; and a collection of tales. With these three substantial books, he inaugurated a career that saw about 100 volumes through the press during the next 40 years.

In 1878 he achieved international renown with his story of an American flirt in Rome, *Daisy Miller*, and further advanced his reputation with *The Europeans* that same year. James's reputation was founded on his versatile studies of "the American girl," and he ended this first phase of his career by producing his masterpiece, *The Portrait of a Lady* (1881), a study of a young woman from Albany who brings to Europe her narrow provincialism and pretensions but also her sense of her own sovereignty, her "free spirit," her refusal to be treated, in the Victorian world, merely as a marriageable object. As a picture of Americans moving in the expatriate society of England and of Italy, this novel has no equal in the history of modern fiction.

Subsequent works were many. In *The Bostonians* (1886) and *The Princess Casamassima* (1886), his subjects were social reformers and revolutionaries. In *The Spoils of Poynton* (1897), *What Maisie Knew* (1897), and *The Turn of the Screw* (1898), he made use of complex moral and psychological ambiguity. *The Wings of the Dove* (1902), *The Ambassadors* (1903), and *The Golden Bowl* (1904) were the great novels of the final phase of his career, all showing a small group of characters in a tense situation, with a retrospective working out, through multiple angles of vision, of their drama. In these late works James resorted to an increasingly allusive prose style, which became dense and charged with symbolic imagery.

In his later years, James lived in retirement in an 18th-century house at Rye in Sussex, though on completion of *The Golden Bowl* he revisited the United States in 1904–05. James had lived abroad for 20 years, and in the interval America had become a great industrial and political power. On his return to England he wrote *The American Scene* (1907), prophetic in its vision of urban doom, spoliation, and pollution of resources and filled with misgivings over the anomalies of a "melting pot" civilization. He devoted three years to rewriting and revising his principal novels and tales for the highly selective "New York Edition," published in 24 volumes. For this edition James wrote 18 significant prefaces, which contain both reminiscence and exposition of his theories of fiction. Throwing his moral weight into Britain's struggle in World War I, James became a British subject in 1915 and received the Order of Merit from King George V.

AUGUST STRINDBERG

(b. Jan. 22, 1849, Stockholm, Swed.—d. May 14, 1912, Stockholm)

August Strindberg was a Swedish playwright, novelist, and short-story writer who combined psychology and Naturalism in a new kind of European drama that evolved into Expressionist drama.

Strindberg's childhood was marred by emotional insecurity, poverty, his grandmother's religious fanaticism, and neglect. He studied intermittently at the University of Uppsala, preparing in turn for the ministry and a career in medicine but never taking a degree. To earn his living, he worked as a freelance journalist in Stockholm, as well as at other jobs that he almost invariably lost. Meanwhile he struggled to complete his first important work, the historical drama *Mäster Olof* (published in 1872), on the theme of the Swedish Reformation, influenced by Shakespeare and by Henrik Ibsen's *Brand*. The Royal Theatre's rejection of *Mäster Olof* deepened his pessimism and sharpened his contempt for official institutions and traditions. For several years he continued revising the play, later recognized as the first modern Swedish drama.

In 1874 he became a librarian at the Royal Library, and in 1875 he met the Finno-Swedish Siri von Essen, then the unhappy wife of an officer of the guards; two years later they married. Their intense but ultimately disastrous relationship ended in divorce in 1891, when Strindberg, to his great grief, lost the custody of their four children. At first, however, marriage stimulated his writing, and in 1879 he published his first novel, *The Red Room*, a satirical account of abuses and frauds in Stockholm society. This was something new in Swedish fiction and made its author nationally famous.

He also wrote more plays, of which *Lucky Peter's Travels* (1881) contains the most biting social criticism. In 1883 Strindberg left Stockholm with his family and for six years moved restlessly about the Continent. Although he was then approaching a state of complete mental breakdown, he produced a great number of plays, novels, and stories. The publication in 1884 of the first volume of his collected stories, *Married*, led to a prosecution for blasphemy. He was acquitted, but the case affected his mind, and he imagined himself persecuted, even by Siri.

He returned to drama with new intensity, and the conflict between the sexes inspired some of the outstanding works written at this time, such as *The Father* (1887), *Miss Julie* (1888), and *The Creditors* (1888). All of these were written in total revolt against contemporary social conventions.

In these bold and concentrated works, he combined the techniques of dramatic Naturalism—including unaffected dialogue, stark rather than luxurious scenery, and the use of stage props as symbols—with his own conception of psychology, thereby inaugurating a new movement in European drama. *The People of Hemsö*, a vigorous novel about the Stockholm skerries (rocky islands), always one of Strindberg's happiest sources of inspiration, was also produced during this intensively creative phase.

The years after his return to Sweden in 1889 were lonely and unhappy. Even though revered as a famous writer who had become the voice of modern Sweden, he was by now an alcoholic unable to find steady employment. In 1892 he went abroad again, to Berlin. His second marriage, to a young Austrian journalist, Frida Uhl, followed in 1893; they finally parted in Paris in 1895.

A period of literary sterility, emotional and physical stress, and considerable mental instability culminated in a kind of religious conversion, the crisis that he described in *Inferno*. During these years Strindberg devoted considerable time to experiments in alchemy and to the study of theosophy. His new faith, colored by mysticism, re-created him as a writer. The immediate result was a drama in three parts, *To Damascus*, in which he depicts himself as "the Stranger," a wanderer seeking spiritual peace and finding it with another character, "the Lady," who resembles both Siri and Frida.

By this time Strindberg had again returned to Sweden, settling first in Lund and then, in 1899, in Stockholm, where he lived until his death. The summers he often spent among his beloved skerries. His view that life is ruled by the "Powers," punitive but righteous, was reflected in a series of historical plays that he began in 1889. Of these, *Gustav Vasa* is the best, masterly in its firmness of construction, characterization, and its vigorous dialogue. In 1901 he married the young Norwegian actress Harriet Bosse; in 1904 they parted, and again Strindberg lost the child, his fifth.

Yet his last marriage, this "spring in winter," as he called it, inspired, among other works, the plays *The Dance of Death* and *A Dream Play*, as well as the charming autobiography *Ensam* ("Alone") and some lyrical poems. Renewed bitterness after his parting from his last wife provoked the grotesquely satirical novel *Svarta Fanor* (1907; "Black Banners"), which attacked the vices and follies of Stockholm's literary coteries, as Strindberg saw them. *Kammarspel* ("Chamber Plays"), written for the little Intima Theater, which Strindberg ran for a time with a young producer, August Falck, embody further developments of his dramatic technique: of these, *The Ghost Sonata* (1907) is the most fantastic, anticipating much in later European drama. His last play, *The Great Highway*, a symbolic presentation of his own life, appeared in 1909. He was ignored in death, as in life, by the Swedish Academy but mourned by his countrymen as their greatest writer. On Swedish life and letters he has exercised a lasting influence.

OSCAR WILDE

(b. Oct. 16, 1854, Dublin, Ire.—d. Nov. 30, 1900, Paris, France)

Oscar Wilde was an Irish wit, poet, and dramatist whose reputation rests on his only novel, *The Picture of Dorian Gray* (1891), and on his comic plays. He was a spokesman for the late 19th-century Aesthetic movement in England, which advocated art for art's sake; and he was the object of celebrated civil and criminal suits involving homosexuality and ending in his imprisonment.

Wilde went, on successive scholarships, to Trinity College, Dublin (1871–74), and Magdalen College, Oxford (1874–78), which awarded him a degree with honors. During these four years, he distinguished himself not only as a classical scholar, a poseur, and a wit but also as a poet by winning the coveted Newdigate Prize in 1878 with a long poem, *Ravenna*.

In the early 1880s, when Aestheticism was the rage and despair of literary London, Wilde established himself in social and artistic circles by his wit and flamboyance. Soon the periodical *Punch* made him the satiric object of its antagonism to the Aesthetes for what was considered their unmasculine devotion to art; and in their comic opera *Patience*, Gilbert and Sullivan based the character Bunthorne, a "fleshly poet," partly on Wilde.

In 1884 Wilde married Constance Lloyd, daughter of a prominent Irish barrister; two children, Cyril and Vyvyan, were born, in 1885 and 1886. Meanwhile, Wilde was a reviewer for the *Pall Mall Gazette* and then became editor of *Woman's World* (1887–89).

In the final decade of his life, Wilde wrote and published nearly all of his major works. In his only novel, *The Picture of Dorian Gray* (published in *Lippincott's Magazine*, 1890, and in book form, revised and expanded by six chapters, 1891), Wilde combined the supernatural elements of the Gothic novel with the unspeakable sins of French decadent fiction. Critics charged immorality despite Dorian's self-destruction; Wilde, however, insisted on the amoral nature of art regardless of an apparently moral ending. Several volumes of essays, stories, and fairy tales also were published in 1891.

But Wilde's greatest successes were his society comedies. Within the conventions of the French "well-made play" (with its social intrigues and artificial devices to resolve conflict), he employed his paradoxical, epigrammatic wit to create a form of comedy new to the 19th-century English theater. His first success, *Lady Windermere's Fan*, demonstrated that this wit could revitalize the rusty machinery of French drama. In the same year, rehearsals of his macabre play *Salomé*, written in French and designed, as he said, to make his audience shudder by its depiction of unnatural passion, were halted by the censor because it contained biblical characters. It was published in 1893, and an English translation appeared in 1894 with Aubrey Beardsley's celebrated illustrations.

A second society comedy, *A Woman of No Importance*, was produced in 1893. In rapid succession, Wilde's final plays, *An Ideal Husband* and *The Importance of Being Earnest*, were produced early in 1895. In the latter, his greatest achievement, the conventional elements of farce are transformed into satiric epigrams—seemingly trivial but mercilessly exposing Victorian hypocrisies:

> *I suppose society is wonderfully delightful. To be in it is merely a bore. But to be out of it simply a tragedy.*
>
> *I never travel without my diary. One should always have something sensational to read in the train.*
>
> *All women become like their mothers. That is their tragedy. No man does. That's his.*

In many of his works, exposure of a secret sin or indiscretion and consequent disgrace is a central design. If life imitated art, as Wilde insisted in his essay "The Decay of Lying" (1889), he was himself approximating the pattern in his reckless pursuit of pleasure. In addition, his close friendship with Lord Alfred Douglas, whom he had met in 1891, infuriated the Marquess of Queensberry, Douglas's father. Accused, finally, by the marquess of being a sodomite, Wilde, urged by Douglas, sued for criminal libel. Wilde's case collapsed, however, when the evidence went against him, and he dropped the suit. Urged to flee to France by his friends, Wilde refused, unable to believe that his world was at an end. He was arrested and ordered to stand trial.

Wilde testified brilliantly, but the jury failed to reach a verdict. In the retrial he was found guilty and sentenced, in May 1895, to two years at hard labor. Most of his sentence was served at Reading Gaol, where he wrote a long letter to Douglas (published in 1905 in a drastically cut version as *De Profundis*) filled with recriminations against the younger man for encouraging him in dissipation and distracting him from his work. In May 1897 Wilde was released and immediately went to France, hoping to regenerate himself as a writer. His only remaining work, however, was *The Ballad of Reading Gaol* (1898), revealing his concern for inhumane prison conditions. He died suddenly of acute meningitis brought on by an ear infection. In his semiconscious final moments, he was received into the Roman Catholic Church, which he had long admired.

ARTHUR RIMBAUD

(b. Oct. 20, 1854, Charleville, France—d. Nov. 10, 1891, Marseille)

Arthur Rimbaud was a French poet and adventurer who won renown among the Symbolist movement and markedly influenced modern poetry.

The provincial son of an army captain, he had begun by age 16 to write violent, blasphemous poems, and he formulated an aesthetic doctrine stating that a poet must become a seer, break down the restraints and controls on personality, and thus become the instrument for the voice of the eternal. At the end of August 1871, on the advice of a friend, Rimbaud sent to the poet Paul Verlaine samples of his new poetry. Verlaine, impressed by their brilliance, summoned Rimbaud to Paris and sent the money for his fare. In a burst of self-confidence, Rimbaud composed *Le Bateau ivre* (written 1871; "The Drunken Boat"), perhaps his finest poem, which displays his astonishing verbal virtuosity and a daring choice of images and metaphors. Once in Paris, he embarked upon a life of drink and debauchery, becoming involved in a homosexual relationship with Verlaine that gave rise to scandal. The two men were soon being seen in public as lovers, and Rimbaud was blamed for breaking up Verlaine's marriage.

In May 1872 Rimbaud was recalled to Paris by Verlaine, who said that he could not live without him. That July Verlaine abandoned his wife and child and fled with Rimbaud to London, where they spent the following winter. During this winter Rimbaud composed a series of 40 prose poems to which he gave the title *Illuminations*. These are his most ambitious attempt to develop new poetic forms from the content of his visions; they try to abolish the distinction between reality and hallucination.

The two poets' relationship was growing so tense and violent that Verlaine became physically ill and mentally disturbed. In April 1873 Rimbaud left him to return to his family, and it was at their farm at Roche, near Charleville, that he began to apply himself to another major work, *Une Saison en enfer* (1873; *A Season in Hell*). A month later Verlaine persuaded Rimbaud to accompany him to London. Rimbaud treated Verlaine with sadistic cruelty, and after more wanderings and quarrels, he rejoined Verlaine in Brussels only to make a last farewell. As he was leaving Verlaine shot him, wounding him in the wrist. Rimbaud was hospitalized, and Verlaine was arrested and sentenced to two years' imprisonment. Rimbaud soon returned to Roche, where he finished *Une Saison en enfer*, which consists of nine fragments of prose and verse. It is a remarkable work of self-confession and psychological examination. In the book's final section, "Adieu" ("Goodbye"), Rimbaud takes a nostalgic backward look at his past life and then moves on; it is a poem sometimes read as Rimbaud's farewell to creative writing.

The rest of Rimbaud's life, from the literary point of view, was silence. In 1875 he set out to see the world, and by 1879 he had crossed the Alps on foot, joined and deserted the Dutch colonial army in the East Indies, visited Egypt, and worked as a laborer in Cyprus, in every instance suffering illness or other hardships. In 1880 he found employment in the service of a coffee trader at Aden (now in Yemen), who sent him to Hārer (now in Ethiopia). He became the first white man to journey into the Ogaden region of Ethiopia, and his report of this expedition was published by France's National Society of Geography in 1884. He made his fortune in Ethiopia, but in early 1891 he returned to France plagued by a tumor on his right knee. The leg was amputated, and cancer was diagnosed; he died several months later.

GEORGE BERNARD SHAW

(b. July 26, 1856, Dublin, Ire.—d. Nov. 2, 1950, Ayot St. Lawrence, Hertfordshire, Eng.)

George Bernard Shaw was an Irish comic dramatist, literary critic, and socialist propagandist and the winner of the Nobel Prize for Literature in 1925.

In 1876 Shaw resolved to become a writer, and he left Ireland to join his mother and elder sister in London. Shaw in his 20s suffered continuous frustration and poverty. He spent his afternoons in the British Museum reading room, writing novels and reading what he had missed at school, and his evenings in search of additional self-education in the lectures and debates that characterized contemporary middle-class London intellectual activities.

His fiction failed utterly. The semiautobiographical and aptly titled *Immaturity* (1879; published 1930) repelled every publisher in London. His next four novels were similarly refused, as were most of the articles he submitted to the press for a decade. Despite his failure as a novelist, Shaw found himself during the 1880s. He became a vegetarian, a socialist, a spellbinding orator, a polemicist, and tentatively a playwright. He became the force behind the newly founded (1884) Fabian Society, a middle-class socialist group that aimed at the transformation of English society not through revolution but through permeation of the country's intellectual and political life. Shaw involved himself in every aspect of its activities, most visibly as editor of one of the classics of British socialism, *Fabian Essays in Socialism* (1889), to which he also contributed two sections.

Eventually, in 1885 the drama critic William Archer found Shaw steady journalistic work. But Shaw truly began to make his mark when he was recruited to the *Saturday Review* as theater critic (1895–98); in that position he used all his wit and polemical powers in a campaign to displace the artificialities and hypocrisies of the Victorian stage with a theater of vital ideas. He also began writing his own plays.

In his first play, *Widowers' Houses* (performed 1892), he emphasized social and economic issues instead of romance, adopting the ironic comedic tone that would characterize all his work. He described his first plays as "unpleasant" because they forced the spectator to face unpleasant facts; these plays include *Mrs. Warren's Profession*, which concerns prostitution; it was written in

1893 but barred from performance until 1902. He followed these with several "pleasant" plays in an effort to find the producers and audiences that his mordant comedies had offended. The first of the second group, *Arms and the Man* (performed 1894), has a Balkan setting and makes lighthearted, though sometimes mordant, fun of romantic falsifications of both love and warfare. *Candida* (performed 1897) and *You Never Can Tell* (performed 1899) are other "pleasant" plays.

Shaw soon became established as a major playwright on the Continent by the performance of his plays there, but, curiously, his reputation lagged in England. It was only with the production of *John Bull's Other Island* (performed 1904) in London, with a special performance for Edward VII, that Shaw's stage reputation was belatedly made in England. Other plays of about the same time include *Man and Superman* (performed 1905), *Major Barbara* (performed 1905), and *The Doctor's Dilemma* (performed 1906), the latter two using high comedy for serious purposes. Possibly Shaw's comedic masterpiece, and certainly his funniest and most popular play, is *Pygmalion* (performed 1913). It was claimed by Shaw to be a didactic drama about phonetics, but the play is a humane comedy about love and the English class system.

World War I was a watershed for Shaw. At first he ceased writing plays. But by the 1920s he had returned to drama, most notably with *Saint Joan* (performed 1923), a chronicle play about Joan of Arc. Acclaim for it led to the awarding of the 1925 Nobel Prize for Literature to Shaw (he refused the award).

Impudent, irreverent, and always a showman, Shaw used his buoyant wit to keep himself in the public eye to the end of his 94 years. He was not merely the best comic dramatist of his time but also one of the most significant playwrights in the English language since the 17th century.

He was also the most trenchant pamphleteer since Swift; the most readable music critic in English; the best theater critic of his generation; a prodigious lecturer and essayist on politics, economics, and sociological subjects; and one of the most prolific letter writers in literature.

ANTON CHEKHOV

(b. Jan. 29 [Jan. 17, Old Style], 1860, Taganrog, Russia—d. July 14/15 [July 1/2], 1904, Badenweiler, Ger.)

Anton Pavlovich Chekhov was a major Russian playwright and master of the modern short story. He is regarded as the outstanding representative of the late 19th-century Russian realist school.

Chekhov, the son of a former serf, became a doctor in 1884. He began his writing career as the author of anecdotes for humorous journals, signing his early work pseudonymously. By 1888 he had become widely popular with a "lowbrow" public and had already produced a body of work more voluminous than all his later writings put together. He had also experimented in serious writing, providing studies of human misery and despair at variance with the frenzied facetiousness of his comic work. Gradually this serious vein absorbed him and soon predominated over the comic.

In 1888, Chekhov published his first work in a leading literary review, *Severny vestnik* ("Northern Herald"). With the work in question—a long story entitled "Steppe"—he at last turned his back on comic fiction. "Steppe," an autobiographical work describing a journey in the Ukraine as seen through the eyes of a child, is the first among more than 50 stories published in a variety of journals and selections between 1888 and his death in 1904.

Chekhov also wrote several profoundly tragic studies at this time. The play *Ivanov* (1887–89) culminates in the suicide of a young man nearer to the author's own age. Together with other works of this period, this play belongs to a group among Chekhov's works that have been called clinical studies. They explore the experiences of the mentally or physically ill in a spirit that reminds one that the author was himself a qualified—and remained a sporadically practicing—doctor.

By the late 1880s many critics had begun to reprimand Chekhov for holding no firm political and social views and for failing to endow his works with a sense of direction. Such expectations irked Chekhov, who was unpolitical and philosophically uncommitted. In early 1890 he suddenly sought relief from the irritations of urban intellectual life by undertaking a one-man sociological expedition to a remote island, Sakhalin.

During the years just before and after his Sakhalin expedition, Chekhov had continued his experiments as a dramatist. His *Wood Demon* (1888–89) is a long-winded and ineptly facetious four-act play, which somehow, by a miracle of art, became converted—largely by cutting—into *Dyadya Vanya* (*Uncle Vanya*), one of his greatest stage masterpieces. The conversion—to a superb study of aimlessness in a rural manor house—took place some time between 1890 and 1896; the play was published in 1897. Other dramatic efforts of the period include several of the uproarious one-act farces known as vaudevilles: *Medved* (*The Bear*), *Predlozheniye* (*The Proposal*), and others.

Chayka (*The Seagull*) was first performed in St. Petersburg in 1896. This four-act drama, misnamed a comedy, was badly received; indeed, it was almost hissed off the stage. Chekhov was greatly distressed and left the auditorium during the second act, having suffered one of the most traumatic experiences of his life and vowing never to write for the stage again. Two years later, however, the play was revived by the newly created Moscow Art Theater, enjoying considerable success and helping to reestablish Chekhov as a dramatist. *The Seagull* is a study of the clash between the older and younger generations as it affects two actresses and two writers, some of the details having been suggested by episodes in the lives of Chekhov's friends.

In March 1897 Chekhov had suffered a lung hemorrhage caused by tuberculosis, symptoms of which had become apparent considerably earlier. Never a successful financial manager, Chekhov attempted to regularize his literary affairs in 1899 by selling the copyright of all his existing works, excluding plays, to a publisher for 75,000 rubles, an unduly low sum.

Chekhov's two last plays—*Tri sestry* (1901; *Three Sisters*) and *Vishnyovy sad* (1904; *The Cherry Orchard*)—were both written for the Moscow Art Theater. But much as Chekhov owed to the theater's two founders, Vladimir Nemirovich-Danchenko and Konstanin Stanislavsky, he remained dissatisfied with such rehearsals and performances of his plays as he was able to witness. In *Three Sisters* Chekhov sensitively portrays the longings of a trio of provincial young women, while in *The Cherry Orchard* he offered a poignant picture of the Russian landowning class in decline, portraying characters who remain comic despite their very poignancy. Less than six months after its first performance Chekhov died of tuberculosis.

Glossary

anecdotal: Based on unscientific reports and observations; describes a scene that depicts a story.

anti-Semitism: Hatred of Jewish people.

blasphemous: Showing disrespect to God or something holy.

didactic: A story written or told in such a way that it teaches the reader/listener a moral.

dramatist: Someone who writes plays.

episodic: Made up of a series of episodes; when a larger story is told through several smaller stories in sequence.

extant: Still in existence.

libel: To write and publish a false statement that represents someone in a negative way.

meter: The rhythmic arrangement of syllables in verse.

novellas: Short narratives with their origins in medieval Italy.

polemic: Describes a controversial opinion that attacks another more popular opinion or doctrine.

prose: Writing that is not poetry.

satire: Something that makes fun of and shows the weaknesses of human nature.

treatise: A formal exposition in writing, generally longer and more specific than an essay.

For More Information

BOOKS

Ashmore, Wayne, and Jennifer Nault. *Mark Twain*. New York, NY: AV2, 2021.

Carroll, Lewis. *Jabberwocky*. Philadelphia, PA: Running Press Kids, 2020.

Dickinson, Emily. *The Poetry of Emily Dickinson*. London, UK: Sirius Publishing, 2023.

Eliot, George. *Silas Marner*. Southampton, UK: Magic Flute Publishing, 2021.

WEBSITES

Berkshire County Historical Society
berkshirehistory.org/herman-melville-arrowhead/melville-in-the-berkshires/
Read about Arrowhead, Herman Melville's home in the Berkshires from 1850 to 1863.

The Mark Twain House and Museum
marktwainhouse.org/about/mark-twain/famous-twain-quotes/
This website offers an amusing collection of some of Mark Twain's many quotes and witticisms.

Poetry Foundation
www.poetryfoundation.org/poets/emily-dickinson
You can find biographical information about Emily Dickinson and a selection of her poetry on this site.

Poets.org
poets.org/poet/charles-baudelaire
Read English translations of poems by the French writer Charles Baudelaire.

Index